Zara Pfeifer

ICC
BERLIN

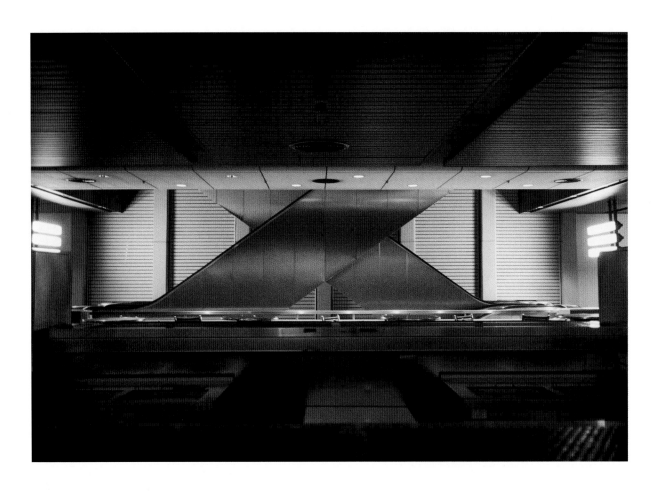

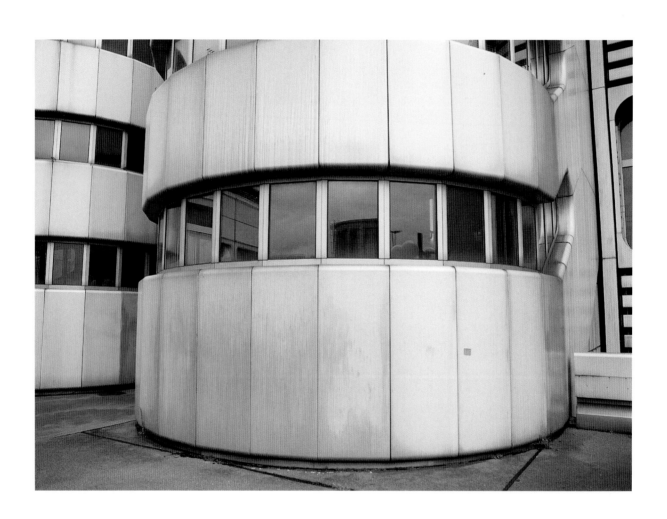

DER SCHLAFENDE RIESE VON WEST-BERLIN

Florian Heilmeyer

Der „Koloss von Witzleben", das „Alu-Monster", der „Panzerkreuzer Charlottenburg", der „Aluminiumdampfer", die „Halle Größenwahn", das „Riesengürteltier" oder – mein Favorit – der „Silberwal": Vielleicht hat kein anderes Gebäude in Berlin je so viele Spitznamen gesammelt wie das Internationale Congress Centrum Berlin, das ICC. Noch immer thront es mächtig und silbrig glänzend auf seiner kleinen Anhöhe zwischen Funkturm und Autobahnkreuz. Eine Ikone der Nachkriegsmoderne West-Berlins. Noch über 40 Jahre nach der Eröffnung am 2. April 1979 ist das ICC dieselbe gigantische futuristische Maschine, die ihresgleichen sucht und nirgends findet. Wahrscheinlich war auch deswegen der Berliner Volksmund, sonst um keinen treffenden Spitznamen verlegen, an dieser Stelle so unentschlossen. Was sollte man mit diesem Wahnsinnsgebäude anfangen, das eher Weltraumkreuzern, Ozeandampfern oder Zeppelindocks verwandt schien denn herkömmlicher Architektur? Seinem verschlissenen Äußeren zum Trotz hat es bis heute nichts von seiner mysteriösen Ausstrahlung verloren. Noch heute fragen Kinder auf den Rücksitzen der vorbeirasenden Autos: „Mama, was ist das?"

Am Urstromtal des 20. Jahrhunderts

„Ähnlich bedeutenden öffentlichen Gebäuden an großen Flüssen europäischer Metropolen, die mit ihrer Längsfront am Stromufer stehen und ihre Öffentlichkeit und Bedeutung demonstrieren, liegt das ICC Berlin mit seiner Ostseite längs neben einem breiten, stromähnlichen Geländeeinschnitt, in dem Autobahnen, die Stadtbahn und Eisenbahnen geführt werden."[1] So schrieben es die beiden Architekten des ICC, Ursulina Schüler-Witte und Ralf Schüler, zur Eröffnung

WEST BERLIN'S SLEEPING GIANT

Florian Heilmeyer

The Giant of Witzleben, the Aluminum Monster, the Battleship Charlottenburg, the Aluminum Steamboat, the Hall of Megalomania, the Great Big Armadillo, or—my favorite—the Silver Whale: perhaps no other building in Berlin has ever garnered so many monikers as the International Congress Centrum Berlin, or ICC. It still stands there today, towering up with a sliver gleam on a small elevation between Berlin's radio tower and a freeway interchange: an icon of postwar modernism in West Berlin. More than forty years after it opened its doors on April 2, 1979, the ICC is still the same gigantic futuristic machine with nothing like it anywhere else. This is probably why Berlin slang—hardly known for its trouble with finding nicknames—proved so indecisive here. What could anyone say about this insane building? A building that was the most expensive in West Germany at the time? A building that seemed more like a spaceship, an ocean liner, or a Zeppelin dock than any conventional architecture? Despite its worn and torn exterior, the building has lost none of its mysterious aura. "Mommy"—you can still hear children say, passing by in the backseat of a car—"What is that?"

A Glacial Valley from the Twentieth Century

"Similar to important public buildings on major rivers in European cities—which are often situated with their longitudinal front facing the river bank, where they proudly claim a space of public significance— the ICC Berlin lies with its eastern side longitudinally next to a wide, river-like cut in the terrain through which freeways, the suburban railway line, and other railroads are routed."[1] This is what the two architects of the ICC, Ursulina Schüler-Witte and Ralf Schüler, wrote in the journal Bauwelt when the ICC was first opened in 1979. Their

1979 in der Bauwelt. Sie griffen damit eine sehr zeittypische Lesart der Berliner Verkehrsströme auf, wie sie Hans Scharoun in seinen Konzepten der „Stadtlandschaft" schon in den 1950er- und 1960er-Jahren formuliert hatte. Speziell seinen grandiosen Entwurf für das Kulturforum hatte Scharoun in landschaftstypologische Elemente unterteilt: Die Staatsbibliothek als Bergrücken, der Kammermusiksaal als Hügel, das (nie gebaute) Gästehaus als Steinterrasse und die Potsdamer Straße als lieblicher Taleinschnitt dazwischen. Witte und Schüler katapultierten diese Idee in eine neue Dimension und erklärten die tosende Schlucht der Stadtautobahn zum Berliner Urstromtal des 20. Jahrhunderts.

Und es passt: Weder Form noch Konstruktion des ICC lassen sich verstehen ohne das Umfeld. 313 Meter lang, 89 Meter breit und bis zu 40 Meter hoch, ringsum mit Aluminium verkleidet, dominiert von vier gewaltigen Fachwerkträgern aus Stahl, zwei an jeder Seite, ebenfalls mit Aluminiumplatten umwickelt. Stünde dieser Silberrücken an einer anderen Stelle der Stadt, er würde sein Umfeld verschlucken und erdrücken; noch auf dem Alexanderplatz wäre dies ein gewaltiger Maßstabssprung. Aber hier, wo die Infrastrukturen der modernen Stadt längst jeden menschlichen Maßstab hinter sich gelassen haben, steht er ganz selbstverständlich leicht erhöht inmitten der vielfach verschlungenen Schlaufen von Schnellstraßen, Brücken und Bahntrassen. Das ICC nimmt das rasante Treiben der ringsum vorbeijagenden Autos, Laster und Eisenbahnen gutmütig in sich auf und führt es – mit klarer Konsequenz – zu neuer Form. Es ist Karosserie, Lokomotive, Maschine und Gebäude zu gleichen Teilen, eine Fortsetzung des Funkturms mit anderen Mitteln. Auch deswegen ist das ICC eine so herausragende architektonische Leistung: Es ist seinem Umfeld eine logische Stadtkrone.

description drew from an interpretation of Berlin's traffic flows that was typical for the time, reflecting ideas that Hans Scharoun had formulated not long before in the 1950s and 60s with his notions of "urban landscape." Scharoun had specifically divided his grandiose plan for the Berlin Kulturforum into elements that he took to be typological for landscapes: the State Library as a ridge, the Chamber Music Hall as a hill, the Guest House (never built) as a stone terrace, and Potsdamer Straße as a lovely valley running between them. Witte and Schüler catapulted this idea into a new dimension, declaring the roaring gorge of the city freeway to be a twentieth-century version of the Berlin Urstromtal—the glacial valley carved across the land at the end of the last ice age.

It's a fitting perspective: neither the form nor the construction of the ICC can be understood without its surroundings. The building stands 313 meters long, 89 meters wide, and up to 40 meters high, clad entirely in aluminum and dominated by four enormous steel truss girders, two on each side, that are also wrapped with aluminum plates. If this silverback beast stood in any other part of the city, it would swallow up and overwhelm its surroundings; even on Alexanderplatz, it would mark a leap in scale. But here, where the infrastructure of the modern city has long since left any human scale behind, it stands very matter-of-factly amid the multiple intertwined loops of expressways, bridges, and railroad tracks. The ICC amiably absorbs the fast-paced crush of the cars, trucks, and railroads rushing by all around, reshaping their energy with rigorous clarity into a new form. It is at once mechanical shell, locomotive, machine, and building, a continuation of the radio tower by other means. And this is another reason why the ICC is such an outstanding architectural achievement: it adorns its surroundings as a fitting city crown.

111

Die Radikalität einer frisch ummauerten Stadt

Das ICC hätte an keiner anderen Stelle so gebaut werden können – und es wäre auch zu keiner anderen Zeit möglich gewesen. Es ist ein Kind der 1960er-Jahre West-Berlins. Die Mauer hatte die Stadt gespalten und es sah nicht so aus, als ob sich an dieser extremen Situation so bald etwas ändern würde. Die eingemauerte Stadthälfte hatte gerade begonnen, sich in ihrer Splendid Isolation einzurichten: Der Raum war knapp, also durften architektonische und stadtplanerische Ideen von außergewöhnlicher Radikalität sein. Aus diesen Jahren stammen die Pläne für das Märkische Viertel, die Gropiusstadt oder das Neue Kreuzberger Zentrum, für die Thermometersiedlung in Lichterfelde, für die Autobahnüberbauung an der Schlangenbader Straße, für den brutalistischen „Mäusebunker" ebenso wie für das großartige Hygiene-Institut in Steglitz.[2]

Dabei gab es ein erstaunlich großes Vertrauen in die Schaffenskraft junger Architekten: Gerade erst hatten 1965 drei junge, völlig unbekannte Hamburger Architekten – Meinhard von Gerkan, Volkwin Marg und Klaus Nickels – mit dem radikalen Konzept eines Drive-in-Flughafens den internationalen Wettbewerb für einen neuen Flughafen in Tegel gewonnen.[3] Unmittelbar danach gewannen im April 1966 Witte und Schüler, noch unverheiratet, den Wettbewerb für die Erweiterung des Messegeländes. Auch sie hatten – wie Gerkan, Marg und Nickels – noch kein einziges gebautes Projekt vorzuweisen. Aus heutiger Sicht erscheint es geradezu atemberaubend, wie sehr die Stadtoffiziellen damals in die Kraft neuer Ideen und deren Umsetzbarkeit vertrauten. Ein vergleichbares Zukunfts- und Jugendvertrauen hat es in Berlin seitdem nicht mehr gegeben.

Beim Wettbewerb für die Messe ging es 1965 um den Bau mehrerer Ausstellungshallen und eines zentralen

The Radicality of a Freshly Walled City

The ICC could not have been built in this way in any other place—nor would it have been possible at any other time. It is a child of 1960s West Berlin. The wall had just divided the city, and by the end of the decade there wasn't much expectation that the extreme situation might change soon. The immured half of the city had only begun to settle into its splendid isolation: space was scarce, permitting ideas for architecture and urban planning of unparalleled radicality. The plans for the Märkisches Viertel, the Gropiusstadt, or the Neues Kreuzberger Zentrum, for the Thermometersiedlung in Lichterfelde, the freeway superstructure on Schlangenbader Straße, the brutalist Mouse Bunker, and the magnificent Institute for Hygiene in Steglitz all date from these years.[2]

Such buildings reflected an astonishing level of confidence in the creative power of young architects: in 1965, for instance, three completely unknown Hamburg architects not more than thirty years old—Meinhard von Gerkan, Volkwin Marg, and Klaus Nickels—had won the international competition for a new airport in Tegel with their radical concept of a drive-in airport.[3] Immediately afterwards, in April 1966, Witte and Schüler (not yet married) won the competition to expand the West Berlin trade fair. Like Gerkan, Marg, and Nickels in the year before, they too had not a single built project to their names. From today's perspective, the trust that city officials placed in the power of new ideas—and in the power of these architects to see them realized—looks breathtaking. A comparable trust in the future, and in the young generation, has not been seen in Berlin since.

The competition for the grounds in 1965 was for the construction of several exhibition halls and a central building. The intention was to reactivate plans from before the war: decades earlier, in 1929/30, city architect Martin Wagner had presented

Kongressgebäudes. Damit griff man Vorkriegspläne wieder auf: Schon 1929/30 hatte Stadtbaurat Martin Wagner zusammen mit dem Architekten Hans Poelzig ein Gesamtkonzept vorgelegt. Das Messegelände wollten sie zu einer großen, expressionistischen Ovalform mit einem Kongresspalast als imposantem Kuppelbau auf kreisrundem Grundriss am nordwestlichen Haupteingang zur Stadt entwickeln. Die Weltwirtschaftskrise und die Machtergreifung der National-sozialisten verhinderten eine Umsetzung, die dem Messegelände heute einen ganz anderen Ausdruck verliehen hätte – jedenfalls wenn man von der ästhetischen Wirkung des Hauses des Rundfunks auf der anderen Straßenseite, das 1930 nach Poelzigs Entwürfen gebaut wurde, auf den Kongresspalast rückfolgern darf. Das Rundfunkgebäude aber blieb der einzig realisierte Bau. Statt Poelzigs Palast wurde von 1935 bis 1937 eine neoklassizistische „Ehrenhalle", stur rechteckig und mit langem, geradem Kolonnadenlauf, als Hauptgebäude der Messe errichtet, entworfen vom NSDAP-treuen Architekten Richard Ermisch.

Der steinernen Schwere wollten Ursulina Witte und Ralf Schüler etwas betont Leichtes entgegenstellen. Dafür erfand Ralf Schüler, gelernter Elektromechaniker mit einem Faible für Konstruktives, einen „ganz neuen Messehallen-Typ"[4]: „Grazile Stahlbeton-Kragarme trugen angehängte, abgestufte Dachkonstruktionen. Zwischen die Hallen konnten farbige Segelflächen gespannt werden. Hierdurch wurde ein heiteres, martkhallenähnliches Ambiente geschaffen."[5] Zwischen diesen Hallen lag das Kongresszentrum als großes Sechseck – vis-à-vis des frisch wiedererrichteten Kastens der Deutschlandhalle –, „teilbar in drei Fünfeck-Säle, überspannt mit einer zeltartigen Dachkonstruktion".[6] Die Modelle lassen erahnen, dass hier mehr Frei Otto entstanden wäre denn Poelzig oder gar Ermisch. Dies war der erste Entwurf fürs ICC. Realisiert wurde davon

an overall concept for an exhibition site together with architect Hans Poelzig. The aim was to develop the trade fair site into a large, expressionistic oval shape, with a congress palace as an imposing domed building on a circular ground plan at the northwestern main entrance to the city. The world economic crisis and rise of the Nazi regime prevented the realization of these ambitious plans, which would have given the exhibition grounds a very different look today—at least if one imagines a Congress Palace here shaped by the aesthetics of the Haus des Rundfunks (House of Broadcasting) across the street, built in 1930 according to Poelzig's designs. The broadcasting building, however, remained the sole structure to be realized. Instead of Poelzig's palace, a neoclassical "Hall of Honor"—stubbornly rectangular, with a long, straight colonnade—was erected from 1935 to 1937 as the main entrance to the exhibition grounds, designed by the architect Richard Ermisch, an opportunistic supporter of Berlin's new Nazi rulers.

Ursulina Witte and Ralf Schüler wanted to counter the heaviness of this monumental stone construction with an emphatic lightness. To do so, Ralf Schüler, a trained electromechanical engineer with a penchant for construction, invented an "entirely new type of exhibition hall":[4] "Graceful reinforced concrete cantilevers supported attached, stepped roof structures. Colored sails could be stretched between the halls. This created a cheerful ambiance reminiscent of a market."[5] Between these halls, the Congress Center was conceived as a large hexagon—directly across from the recently rebuilt box of the Deutschlandhalle: "divisible into three pentagon-shaped halls, and covered by a tent-like roof construction."[6] The models suggest that this would have been more Frei Otto than Poelzig or even Ermisch. This was the first design for the ICC, but none of it was built. After the competition was decided, there were no funds available for construction.

nichts. Nach dem Wettbewerbsentscheid standen keine Gelder für den Bau zur Verfügung.

Erst 1969 kam neuer Schwung in die Planungen. Wirtschaftsvertreter und Stadtpolitiker stellten plötzlich fest, dass es in West-Berlin an einem Kongresszentrum von internationalem Format und mit einem größeren Fassungsvermögen als Hugh Stubbins' Kongresshalle im Tiergarten fehle. Allerdings sollte der Neubau jetzt nicht mehr versteckt hinter dem Messegelände stehen, wie im Wettbewerb noch gefordert, sondern so, „dass er für eine breite Öffentlichkeit ständig sichtbar sei".[7] Im Frühjahr beauftragte die Stadt die Architekten mit einer Untersuchung von vier möglichen Standorten rund um den nördlichen Haupteingang am Hammarskjöldplatz. Laut Schüler-Witte hätten die Architekten am liebsten direkt vor Ermischs „Ehrenhalle" gebaut, die sie als Bühnenhaus (!) in ihren Neubau integrieren wollten. So hätten sie sich gleichzeitig auf die Pläne von Wagner und Poelzig beziehen und die faschistische Germania-Ästhetik von Ermischs Kolonnadenhalle gründlich zerbröseln können – indem sie die Halle schlicht verschluckt hätten. Zu einer so radikal antifaschistischen Architektur aber konnte sich der Berliner Senat nicht entschließen. Und so wurde der große Parkplatz zwischen Funkturm und Stadtautobahn gewählt. Aus Sicht der Architekten die ungünstigste der vier Möglichkeiten.

Zweiteiliger Maßanzug

Die Probleme mit dem Grundstück beschreibt Schüler-Witte so: „Dieser in vielerlei Hinsicht ungünstige Standort war weitaus zu schmal, um dort [unseren] Wettbewerbsentwurf – selbst in abgewandelter Form – errichten zu können. Auch war er vom Verkehrslärm stark belastet, insbesondere durch die Schwerlasttransporte auf dem Messedamm und die Erz-Züge auf der Bahntrasse neben der Stadtautobahn. Zudem gab es

In 1969, the planning got a new boost. Representatives from business and local politicians suddenly realized that what was missing in West Berlin was precisely an internationally prominent convention center with more capacity than Hugh Stubbins's Congress Hall in the Tiergarten. Yet there was no longer any intention of hiding the new architecture behind the exhibition grounds, as the competition had required. Now, it was to be "constantly visible to a broad public."[7] That spring, the city commissioned Schüler and Witte to study four possible sites around the main northern entrance at Hammarskjöldplatz. According to Schüler-Witte, the architects would have preferred to build directly in front of Ermisch's "Hall of Honor," which they wanted to integrate into their new building, making it just one of the new building's several event spaces. This would have allowed them to keep a reference to the plans made by Wagner and Poelzig while also thoroughly demolishing—by swallowing!—the fascist Germania aesthetic of Ermisch's colonnaded structure. But the Berlin Senate proved incapable of making such a choice, and so the large parking lot between the radio tower and the city freeway was the solution. From the architects' point of view, this was the least favorable of the four options.

A Two-Piece Custom Suit

Schüler-Witte describes the problems with the location: "Unfavorable in many respects, the site was far too narrow for the construction of [our] competition design, even in a modified form. It was also heavily affected by the din of traffic, especially from the transport of heavy goods on the Messedamm and the trains carrying ore that ran on the railway line next to the city freeway. Moreover, there was hardly any space on the site for a forecourt of adequate size … [or] to accommodate private traffic and taxis and shuttle buses at street level."[8] So once again, inventiveness was required.

114

kaum Raum auf dem Grundstück für einen Vorplatz in angemessener Größe […] [oder] zur Aufnahme des Individualverkehrs und der Taxen sowie der Zubringerbusse auf Straßenniveau."8 Es war also erneut Erfindungsgeist gefragt.

Statt eines flächig ausgebreiteten Kongresszentrums musste das Programm nun in die Höhe gestapelt werden. So wurde das ICC zu einem etwa zwölfgeschossigen Volumen auf rechteckigem Grundriss, der das Grundstück fast maximal ausnutzt und nur nach Norden, zur Kantstraße und zum S-Bahnhof, einen Vorplatz lässt. Mit diesem Vorplatz erhielten Schüler-Witte und Schüler auch die Sichtachse von der S-Bahn zur Rotunde und zum Funkturm. Das ICC, die große Maschine, steht, von der Stadt aus gesehen, links im Bild und weist mit seinem enormen Körper in Richtung AVUS.

Dieser große Körper ist in zwei klar unterscheidbare Teile gegliedert: Der Hauptkörper, das „innere Gebäude", ist eine Stahlbetonkonstruktion. Er besteht zuerst aus zwei Reihen von je dreizehn kräftigen Säulen, jede mit 2,5 Metern im Durchmesser, die in Längsrichtung das Hauptgebäude tragen. Sie sind auch im Innern immer wieder als weiß gestrichene, aber unverkleidete Betonsäulen zu finden. Zwischen ihnen liegen dreizehn 60 Meter lange Querwände aus Stahlbeton wie Schotten eines Schiffs. In dieser Grundstruktur befinden sich alle Veranstaltungssäle und -räume sowie die weiten, offenen Foyerlandschaften mit ihren geschickt ineinander verschachtelten Terrassen, Balkonen, Brücken und Stegen, die Blicke kreuz und quer durch den Innenraum ermöglichen. So lassen sich die anderen Besucher im Haus beobachten, wie sie in die Räume hinein und aus ihnen heraus spazieren und wie die Rolltreppen sie magisch auf- und abwärts schweben lassen. Bis zu 20.000 Kongressteilnehmer kann dieses Haus aufnehmen, die weiten Foyerflächen können für parallele Veranstaltungen jeweils anders unterteilt oder miteinander kombiniert werden.

Instead of a convention center spread out over a large area, the plan was now to stack the space required upwards. This is how the ICC became a volume approximately twelve stories high on a rectangular ground plan that almost entirely utilizes the site, leaving a forecourt only to the north, toward Kantstraße and the station for the S-Bahn, or city railway. With this forecourt, Schüler-Witte and Schüler also kept the visual axis from the city to the older rotunda of the Messe buildings and to the radio tower intact. The ICC—as a gigantic machine powering the fairground—stands on the left in this postcard view from the city, pointing with its enormous body in the direction of the AVUS.

This great bulk is divided into two clearly distinguishable parts. The main body, the "inner building," is a reinforced concrete structure. It consists first of two rows of thirteen stout columns, each 2.5 meters in diameter, that longitudinally support the main building. Inside, these supports are also repeatedly visible as white-painted but unclad concrete columns. Between them, one finds thirteen sixty-meter-long transverse walls made of reinforced concrete, like the bulkheads of a ship. This basic structure houses all the building's event halls and convention spaces, as well as the wide, open foyer landscapes with their deftly interlocking terraces, balconies, bridges, and walkways that allow views crisscrossing the interior. Visitors to the building can thus see each other as they walk in and out of the spaces, or as they appear to magically float on the escalators from level to level. This building can accommodate events with up to 20,000 participants, and the wide foyer areas can be subdivided differently or combined for parallel events. Inside, the ICC resembles a beehive.

This entire construction rests on elastic neoprene bearings, which compensate for the constant trembling from the surrounding area and thus seal off the interior against sound and vibration. This sound insulation is even more effective

Das ICC gleicht im Innern einem Bienenstock.

Diese gesamte Konstruktion liegt auf elastischen Neoprenlagern. Sie gleichen die Erschütterungen der Umgebung aus und schotten das Innere so gegen Schall und Vibration ab. Diese Schallisolation gelingt umso besser, da es einen zweiten Gebäudeteil gibt: die große Aluminiumhaut, die den Hauptteil des Gebäudes umfängt. Diese Haut wird von zwölf deutlich sichtbaren Querspanten umfangen, die an den vier ebenfalls außen liegenden, übergroßen Fachwerkträgern hängen, zwei zu jeder Seite. Die Stahlkonstruktion der mächtigen Träger wird vollständig von Aluminiumplatten ummantelt. Jeder dieser Träger liegt wieder auf zwei Stahlbetonstützen, deren Stützenköpfe, als dunklere Elemente in der silbernen Außenhaut deutlich betont, ebenfalls auf elastischen Neoprenlagern liegen. Diese Hülle bildet die seitlichen Außenwände und das gesamte Dach. Die Saaldecken über den beiden größten Veranstaltungsräumen auf der obersten Ebene des ICC gehören ebenfalls zu diesem zweiten Gebäudeteil, inklusive aller Beleuchtungstrassen, Lautsprecher und den in die Decke eingehängten Übersetzerkabinen. Diese beiden großen Bauteile, Hülle und Inhalt, sind an keiner Stelle fest miteinander verbunden, sodass weder Schall noch Schwingungen übertragen werden können. Es ist eine Konstruktionsart, wie man sie sonst vor allem von Autobahnbrücken kennt. Auch sonst gestalteten Schüler-Witte und Schüler die Elemente des Kongresszentrums innen wie außen eher mit Blick auf Autos, Flugzeuge oder Lokomotiven, nur größer: Die Formen der vertikalen Stahlbetonstützen, welche die Fachwerkträger halten, bleiben vollständig in den nach außen geschwungenen Doppeltreppenhäusern verborgen, die an Zylinder denken lassen. In die auffällige Lücke zwischen den Trägerpaaren an jeder Seite setzten die Architekten je zwei gewaltige Ansaugstutzen der Luftanlage. Wie übergroße Schnorchel erinnern sie an

thanks to a second part of the building: the large aluminum skin that encloses the main structure. This skin is enveloped by twelve clearly visible transverse ribs hanging from the four oversized trusses, also on the exterior, two on each side. The steel structure formed by these mighty beams is completely encased in aluminum plates. Each of these girders again rests on two reinforced concrete columns whose column heads, clearly emphasized as darker elements in the building's silver skin, also rest on elastic neoprene bearings. This envelope forms the side exterior walls and the entire roof. Even the hall ceilings above the two largest event rooms on the top level of the ICC belong to this second part of the building, including all lighting lines, loudspeakers, and translator booths suspended in the ceiling. These two large components, shell and contents, are not firmly connected to each other at any point, thus preventing the transmission of both sound and vibration. It is a type of construction otherwise known mainly from highway bridges, and Schüler-Witte and Schüler similarly designed all other elements of the convention center—inside and out—with more of a view toward cars, airplanes, or locomotives, only bigger. Reminiscent of cylinders, the outwardly curved double staircases hide the shapes of the vertical reinforced concrete columns holding the trusses. In the conspicuous gap between the pairs of beams on each side, the architects placed two enormous air intakes. Like oversized snorkels, they evoke ocean liners or racing cars. Aluminum and concrete also dominate the interior, along with the curved neon lights and drop-leaf display panels of the ICC's proprietary wayfinding system. The association with spaceships and airports was practically foisted on visitors. Remember: Star Trek had been running on ZDF since 1972, and the first of George Lucas's Star Wars films had been shown in German theaters just two years before the ICC opened.

The idea of separating the shell from the core becomes impossible to miss when

Ozeandampfer oder Rennwagen. Auch im Innern dominieren Aluminium und Beton, dazu kommen die gebogenen Neonröhren und die Fallblattanzeigetafeln des ICC-eigenen Leitsystems. Die Assoziation mit Raumschiffen und Flughäfen wurde den Besuchern förmlich aufgedrängt. Man muss bedenken: Star Trek lief seit 1972 im ZDF, die erste Episode von George Lucas' Star-Wars-Trilogie war zwei Jahre vor der Eröffnung des ICC in den Kinos zu sehen.

Die Idee einer Trennung von Hülle und Kern wird überdeutlich beim Blick auf die beiden Giebelseiten des ICC. Die Architekten zogen nach Süden und Norden zwei Gebäudeteile aus dem Inneren ins Freie: im Süden, zum Autobahnkreuz, das Parkhaus; nach Norden die Büros, Werkstätten und das Restaurant Pullmann im obersten Geschoss, die dadurch allesamt zugleich mehr Tageslicht erhalten. Sie bilden über dem Haupteingang ein Vordach, lassen diesen allerdings auch dunkler und niedriger wirken. Ringsum bleibt eine breite, dunkle Fuge zur Hülle deutlich sichtbar. Überhaupt ist dieser Vorplatz ein seltsamer Ort geworden, was nur teilweise an der Architektur des ICC liegt. Als windige, vom Verkehr umtoste Insel ist es eine unwirtliche Stelle, an der man ungern stehen bleibt. Eher können sich die Besucher hier noch einmal kräftig vom Verkehr umspülen lassen, bevor sie ins stille, dunkle Innere flüchten. Dessen durch die elastischen Lager vollständig von der Umgebung entrückte Stille ist umso bemerkenswerter. Staunend steht man vor den übergroßen Panoramafenstern auf der ersten Ebene und blickt auf den Tag und Nacht tosenden, aber nun tonlosen Verkehr. Ein geradezu unheimlicher Effekt.

Schatzkammern im Innern

Was von außen allerdings nicht zu sehen ist: Das ICC ist ein Gesamtkunstwerk. Denn der wahre Schatz sind nicht allein die silbern schimmernde Hülle und die technischen Meisterleistungen seiner Konstruktion, sondern auch der

one is looking at the two gable ends of the ICC. To the south and north, the architects moved two parts of the building from the interior into the open—to the south, the parking garage facing the freeway interchange; and to the north, the offices, workshops, and a restaurant, Pullmann, on the top floor—which flooded all these spaces with more daylight. Over the main entrance, they form a canopy, though they also make it look darker and lower. A wide, dark joint to the shell remains clearly visible all around. This forecourt has become a strange place in many ways, only some of which have to do with the architecture of the ICC. As a windy island amid the urban roar, it is an inhospitable location where people are reluctant to spend time. Visitors can instead experience one last wave of traffic swirling around the site before they escape into the hushed, dimmed interior. The silence of this inner space, completely removed from the surroundings by the elastic bearings, is thus all the more remarkable. Standing in amazement in front of the oversized panoramic windows on the first level, one looks out over traffic flowing by day and night, now stripped of any sound. It's an almost uncanny effect.

The Treasure Chambers Inside

There is something that cannot be seen from the outside, though: the ICC is a Gesamtkunstwerk. Its real treasure is not only the shimmering silver shell and the technical feats of its construction, but also the idiosyncratic character of its interiors and their furnishings. Coming from the forecourt in the north or the parking garage in the south, one enters the boulevard, as it is called, on the first floor through double swing doors: a 180-meter-long foyer zone that stretches through the entire main building. An open information counter stands in the center, gleaming in silver, too. A split-level construction opens to both long sides, preventing the space, which is almost

eigensinnige Charakter seiner Innenräume und deren Ausstattung. Vom Vorplatz im Norden oder vom Parkhaus im Süden betritt man durch die Doppelschwingtüren den „Boulevard" im Erdgeschoss: eine 180 Meter lange Foyerzone, die sich durch das gesamte Hauptgebäude streckt. Mittig steht ein silbern glänzender, offener Informationstresen. Zu beiden Längsseiten öffnet sich eine Split-Level-Konstruktion, die den vom Tageslicht fast völlig abgeschlossenen Raum nicht klaustrophobisch wirken lässt. Ein paar Stufen führen auf der gesamten Länge zu den tiefer liegenden Garderoben, dahinter sind die Zugänge zu den Waschräumen und Toiletten verborgen. Glänzende Rolltreppen schreiben, immer als Paar, Diagonalen in den Raum; sie führen hinauf zu den oberen Foyerflächen. Hier empfängt die Besucher eine kunstvoll ineinander geschachtelte Raumlandschaft aus Treppen, Balkonen, Brücken, Terrassen, kleinen Plätzen und weiten Korridoren. Es sind Räume zum Flanieren und zur gemächlichen Begegnung vor, zwischen und nach den Veranstaltungen. Eine Vielzahl unterschiedlicher Routen ist möglich zu den insgesamt 80 verschiedenen Veranstaltungsräumen in allen Größen und Formen, die sich zu 28 Veranstaltungsarten und für Teilnehmerzahlen von 20 bis 9.000 kombinieren lassen. Denn der Treibstoff dieser Maschine, das waren immer schon die Menschen, das Publikum. Und damit dieser Treibstoff möglichst reibungslos durch das Innere gleiten kann, hatte der Berliner Künstler Frank Oehring für das ICC ein atemberaubendes gebäudeinternes Leitsystem entwickelt, das mit allerlei mechanischen Anzeigen und den blauen und roten Neonröhren die Besucher durchs Haus lotste wie Blutkörperchen durch Arterien und Venen. In loser Reihe wurden außerdem merkwürdige, übergroße Roboterköpfe verteilt, die sich beim Nähertreten als Informations- und Orientierungssäulen entpuppten.

Die Kombinationsmöglichkeiten der Räume und Säle finden ihren spektakulären

completely closed off from daylight, from feeling claustrophobic. A few steps lead along the entire length to the lower-lying coat checks, which also hide the entrances to the restrooms. Bright escalators, always in pairs, trace diagonals in the space, leading up to the upper foyer areas. Here, visitors are greeted by an artfully nested spatial landscape of staircases, balconies, bridges, terraces, smaller seating areas, and wide corridors. These are spaces where visitors can take time to stroll and enjoy leisurely encounters before, between, and after events. A plethora of paths can be taken to reach the 80 different event spaces of all shapes and sizes, which can be combined to create 28 types of events, for participant numbers ranging from 20 to 9,000. The fuel for this machine, after all, has always been the people, the public. And to ensure that this fuel can flow through the interior as smoothly as possible, Berlin artist Frank Oehring developed a unique wayfinding system for the ICC's inner spaces that used a suite of mechanical displays, along with its now-famous blue and red neon lights, to guide visitors through the building just as blood cells flow through arteries and veins. Strange, oversized robot heads—clear references to Darth Vader's stormtroopers in Star Wars?—were also distributed throughout the space in loose rows; when approached, they turned out to be information and orientation pillars.

The possibilities for combining these spaces and halls reach a spectacular climax in the two largest halls on the top level. With its main floor and balcony, Hall 1 offers 5,000 seats, each of them fabricated according to a custom design with a folding seat and table, reading lamp, luggage net, audio access, and built-in ashtray. For smaller events, the ceiling can be lowered; in this case, the balcony disappears. Hall 2 is a mirror image of Hall 1, and its more steeply sloped, three-tiered seating area can hold an audience of 2,000. This entire seating structure hangs from the ceiling on heavy red steel chains and can be fully

Gipfel in den zwei größten Sälen auf der obersten Ebene: Saal 1 bietet mit Parkett und Rang 5.000 Sitzplätze, jeder einzelne eine Spezialanfertigung mit Klappsitz und -tisch, Leselampe, Gepäcknetz, Audiozugang und fest eingebautem Aschenbecher. Für kleinere Veranstaltungen kann die Decke heruntergefahren werden, dann verschwindet der Rang. Saal 2 liegt dem Saal 1 spiegelverkehrt gegenüber, seine dreigeteilte, steilere Tribüne bietet 2.000 Sitzplätze. Diese Tribüne hängt an schweren roten Stahlketten von der Decke und kann auf Knopfdruck vollständig in die Decke hochgeklappt werden. Dann entsteht ein weiter, flacher Saal mit Holzdielung, der für Banketts mit bis zu 4.000 Personen Platz bietet. Das Restaurant grenzt unmittelbar an den Saal an. Obendrein kann die Bühne zwischen den Sälen zu beiden Seiten geöffnet werden, sodass Veranstaltungen mit bis zu 9.000 Teilnehmern um eine Mittelbühne möglich sind. Der Brite Cedric Price hatte in den 1960er-Jahren die Idee eines „Fun Palace" formuliert, eines vollständig verstellbaren Bühnengebäudes, das in wenigen Minuten für jede vorstellbare Veranstaltungsart hätte umgebaut werden können. Es ist nicht überliefert, ob er je im ICC war. Falls ja, dürfen wir annehmen, dass es ihn begeistert hätte.

Aus Mangel an Treibstoff

Heute aber steht das ICC leer. Das ICC ist zwar Eigentum des Landes Berlin, exklusiver Betreiber ist aber die Messe GmbH. Diese organisiert als hundertprozentige Tochtergesellschaft des Landes den Betrieb des Messegeländes, also auch die damit verbundenen Kongresse. Freundlich gesagt ist das eine für das ICC etwas unglückliche Konstellation, denn die Messegesellschaft hatte schon seit der Jahrtausendwende immer wieder über die hohen Betriebskosten des ICC lamentiert, die sie nicht zu tragen in der Lage sei – obwohl das ICC stets bestens

raised into the ceiling at the push of a button. This produces a wide, flat hall with a wooden floor that can accommodate banquets with up to 4,000 people. The restaurant is directly adjacent to the hall. And to top it off, the stage between the halls can be opened on both sides, allowing events with up to 9,000 attendees to take place around a center stage. In the 1960s, the British architect Cedric Price had formulated the idea of a "Fun Palace," a fully adjustable stage building able to be converted in a matter of minutes to host any kind of event imaginable. We don't know whether he ever visited the ICC. But we can guess he would have found it very exciting.

A Shortage of Fuel

Today, though, the ICC stands empty. The building is owned by the state of Berlin, but the company Messe GmbH functions as its exclusive operator—a wholly owned subsidiary of the city that manages the entire fairground's operations, including the congresses for which the ICC was designed. To put it mildly, this is a somewhat unfortunate constellation for the ICC. Over the past twenty years, Messe GmbH has warned again and again about the ICC's high operating costs, which it says it cannot profitably bear even though the ICC has always been fully booked and regularly received national and international awards from congress and trade fair organizers. In the end, the operating company won out over opposition in the Berlin state government and was able to erect a largely faceless, presumably cheap-to-clean new building called the CityCube. When this building opened in April 2014, the ICC closed its doors.

Berlin's local politicians had no success in preventing Messe GmbH's withdrawal, or in countering it with a new use concept for the ICC and the enormous public treasure it represents. On the contrary, the discussions have been marked by a confusing lack of transparency. It is not

ausgebucht war und regelmäßig nationale und internationale Auszeichnungen von Kongress- und Messeveranstaltern erhielt. Letztlich setzte sich die Messegesellschaft gegen die Landespolitik durch und bekam einen weitgehend gesichtslosen, vermutlich günstig zu reinigenden Neubau namens CityCube neben der inzwischen abgerissenen Deutschlandhalle – ungefähr dort, wo auch Schüler-Witte und Schüler ihr erstes sechseckiges Kongresszentrum platziert hätten. Die letzte offizielle Veranstaltung im ICC fand im April 2014 statt.

Die Berliner Politik hat es weder vermocht, den Rückzug der Messe aufzuhalten, noch ihm eine neue Nutzungsidee fürs ICC als gewaltigem öffentlichem Schatz entgegenzusetzen. Ganz im Gegenteil herrscht eine verwirrende Heimlichtuerei, sodass selbst die Kosten einer seit Jahren dringend anstehenden Sanierung und Modernisierung völlig unklar sind. Da die Bestandsaufnahmen – auch die im öffentlichen Auftrag – weitestgehend nicht veröffentlicht werden, geistern allerlei nicht überprüfbare Zahlen durch die Öffentlichkeit. Die Gerüchte über eine angebliche Asbestbelastung konnten zwar inzwischen – unter anderem durch eine sehr engagierte Ursulina Schüler-Witte – widerlegt werden. Die letzte gründliche Fassadenreinigung fand 1998 statt. Für die Gesamtsanierung wurden erst 180 Millionen Euro geschätzt, dann 250 oder 350 Millionen Euro; auch Kosten von 600 oder 900 Millionen Euro wurden bereits genannt. Nachprüfbar ist davon aufgrund der fehlenden Unterlagen und der Schweigsamkeit der Berliner Behörden fast nichts.[9] Klar ist, dass die Messe Berlin wenig Mittel in die Instandhaltung des Gebäudes investierte, das sie gleichzeitig voll auslastete. Hierfür müsste sie eigentlich stärker in die Verantwortung genommen werden – immerhin gehört sie zu den profitabelsten öffentlichen Unternehmen des Landes Berlin.

Die Größe des ICC ist dabei Segen und Fluch. Segen ist sie, weil ein Abriss kaum je zur Debatte stand – er wäre schlicht

even clear what the costs might be for the renovation and modernization that have been so urgently needed for years (and for which Messe GmbH has refused to pay). Since almost none of the studies that have been prepared have ever been published, including those commissioned by public authorities, what we find circulating in the media are all kinds of unverifiable figures. At least it has been possible to publicly refute the rumors about the supposed asbestos contamination of the building, in no small part due to tireless efforts of Ursulina Schüler-Witte herself. The last thorough cleaning of the facade was in 1998. A first estimate for a complete renovation was 180 million euros, then 250 or 350 million. But costs of 600 or 900 million euros have also circulated in the press. Almost none of these numbers can be checked given the lack of documentation and the tight-lipped stance of the Berlin authorities.[9] It is clear that Messe Berlin has invested few resources in maintaining the building, even as it was employed to full capacity. The company should shoulder more financial responsibility here—which it certainly could, as one of the most profitable state-owned companies in Berlin.

In this regard, the size of the ICC is both a blessing and a curse. It is a blessing because demolition has hardly been up for debate: tearing the building down would simply be too expensive, especially since it seems no one has any ideas how the unattractive site could be put to better use than with this brilliant building. Yet size is also a curse, in that Berlin's politicians have retreated into apathy in the face of so enormous a challenge. New studies and surveys have been commissioned, many times over; workshops have been held, and competitions for ideas have been announced for private investors. But nothing has ever been decided. In 2019, the cost of maintaining the building even without any use was reported at 1.8 million euros per year.[10] The lease agreement still in force requires Messe Berlin to pay these expenses. In a rational world, then, all

zu teuer, zumal es an Ideen fehlt, wie das unattraktive Grundstück denn besser zu nutzen wäre als mit diesem brillanten Gebäude. Gleichzeitig ist die Größe Fluch, da sich die Berliner Politik angesichts der Dimension der Aufgabe bislang in Apathie flüchtet. Zwar wurden immer wieder neue Studien und Untersuchungen beauftragt, Workshops veranstaltet und Ideenwettbewerbe für private Investoren ausgeschrieben. Nur entschieden wurde nichts. 2019 wurden die Kosten für den Stillstandsbetrieb mit 1,8 Millionen Euro pro Jahr angegeben.[10] Aufgrund des noch gültigen Pachtvertrags muss die Messe für diese Kosten aufkommen. In einer rationalen Welt sollten also alle Beteiligten ein Interesse daran haben, möglichst rasch Klarheit über die Kosten zu bekommen, um dann sofort ein realistisches Nachnutzungsszenario zu erarbeiten. Stattdessen werden Entscheidungen immer wieder vertagt. Die zwischenzeitlichen Nutzungen als Geflüchtetenunterkunft 2015, als Erstaufnahmestelle 2017 und als Impfzentrum 2020 zeigen keine dauerhaft sinnvolle Perspektive.

Too big to …?

Ist das ICC zu groß für Berlin? Die Kunst- und Kulturszene, die ja gerne übernimmt, wenn die Berliner Politik gerade nicht weiterweiß, denkt darüber anders. So haben sich in den letzten Jahren Initiativen gebildet, die für eine Weiternutzung des ICC als öffentliches Kunst-, Kultur- und Kongresszentrum eintreten, darunter auch die Initiative „ICCC – International Center for Contemporary Culture"[11] um das Berliner Bureau N und einen privaten Investor, der bereit gewesen wäre, mit öffentlicher Beteiligung eine größere Summe in die Wiederherstellung des ICC zu stecken. Auch Zara Pfeifer und ich waren und sind Teil dieser Initiative, und so sind wir 2014 ein erstes Mal gemeinsam durch das damals ganz leere Haus flaniert. Leider hat uns das Land Berlin auf das eingereichte Konzept nie eine offizielle Antwort gegeben.

parties would have an interest in getting a clear picture of costs as quickly as possible so that a realistic scenario for a subsequent use can be worked out without delay. What keeps happening instead is that decisions are postponed. The interim uses as a refugee shelter in 2015, as a welcome center for refugees in 2017, and as a vaccination center in 2020 offer no sensible long-term prospects.

Too big to …?

Is the ICC too big for Berlin? Berlin's art and culture scene, which never has a problem taking over when Berlin politicians are at a loss about what to do, has different ideas. In recent years, for example, initiatives have repeatedly been launched to advocate for the continued use of the ICC as a public center for arts, culture, and congresses. One of these is the ICCC— International Center for Contemporary Culture,[11] formed around the Berlin-based Bureau N and a private investor who would have been willing to invest a significant sum in the restoration of the ICC if this were accompanied by public funds. Zara Pfeifer and I have been, and still are, part of this initiative, and it was in this capacity that we strolled together through the building for the first time in 2014. At that time, it was completely empty. Unfortunately, we never received an official response from the state of Berlin to the use concept we submitted.

Zara Pfeifer's 2014 photographs primarily aimed to document the current state of the ICC. As part of the ICCC Initiative, it was important to be able to convey a picture of the ICC's futuristic, exotic interior worlds, which need investment for renovation but are generally in good shape. Thousands of people pass by the convention center every day in cars and trains, yet hardly any of them know anything about the magical spaces it holds. Even many people who once attended conventions or concerts here often think that the building has been emptied out. And this is one of the greatest dangers

Zara Pfeifers Aufnahmen sollten 2014 vor allem den Ist-Zustand des ICC dokumentieren. Im Rahmen der ICCC-Initiative war es wichtig, den zwar zuwendungsbedürftigen, aber insgesamt guten Erhalt der futuristisch-exotischen Innenwelten des ICC zeigen zu können. Denn obwohl so viele Menschen jeden Tag in Autos und Eisenbahnen am Kongresszentrum vorbeifahren, weiß doch kaum jemand von dessen inneren Zauberwelten. Selbst die, die hier einst Kongresse oder Konzerte besucht haben, glaubten, dass das ICC längst ausgeräumt sei. Und das ist eine der größten aktuellen Gefahren für dieses Gesamtkunstwerk, dessen Gestaltung von der äußeren Hülle bis zum letzten Garderobenhaken aufeinander abgestimmt ist: dass es zu viel von seinem Innenleben verlieren könnte, wenn – wie bereits ernsthaft diskutiert – eine Shoppingmall oder ein Casino mit Autobahnanschluss daraus werden sollte. Diverse Nutzungsvorschläge, die durch die Presse geisterten, setzten einen vollständigen inneren Abriss voraus, um das Raumschiff wieder weltraumfähig zu machen. Dem muss energisch widersprochen werden. Tatsächlich handelt es sich – paradoxerweise gerade dank der so lange ausstehenden Modernisierung – um eine echte Zeitkapsel, die uns weitgehend originalgetreu erhalten ist. Zum Glück hat dies auch das Landesdenkmalamt inzwischen erkannt und das ICC 2019 insgesamt unter Denkmalschutz gestellt, das Äußere wie sein Inneres.[12] Dass eine kulturelle Nachnutzung nicht nur mit wenigen Mitteln möglich ist, sondern darüber hinaus Spaß machen könnte, haben die Berliner Festspiele jüngst gezeigt. Ihnen ist es erstmals gelungen, das Land und die Messe Berlin zu überzeugen, das Haus für ein zehntägiges Kunst- und Performance-Festival zu öffnen, benannt nach einem David-Bowie-Song: „The Sun Machine Is Coming Down" öffnete den Silberwal im Oktober 2021 ein erstes Mal als zusammenhängend bespieltes Haus der freien Künste.[13] So konnte eine breite

currently facing this Gesamtkunstwerk, its design so carefully coordinated from its outer shell to its coat hooks: that it might lose all or too much of its inner life if—as has been seriously discussed—it were to become a shopping mall or a casino. Various proposals for using the building that have circulated in the press presupposed a complete internal demolition in order to make the spaceship spaceworthy again. This idea must be vigorously opposed. The modernization that has been postponed for so long has ironically left the building as a true time capsule preserved for us in its nearly original form. It is fortunate that the Berlin Monument Authority, too, has now recognized this fact, placing the ICC as a whole, both the exterior and its interior, under monument protection in 2019.[12] And the Berliner Festspiele have recently shown that cultural reuse is not only possible even with limited resources—it can be fun, too. They broke ground in successfully convincing the state of Berlin and Messe Berlin to open up the building for an art and performance festival, named after a David Bowie song: over a period of ten days in October 2021, "The Sun Machine Is Coming Down" became the first event to open up the Silver Whale to the public, as a curated site-specific installation of multiple art projects and performances.[13] One consequence was that the many festival visitors could see for themselves that the building was hardly as ruined and dilapidated on the inside as it might appear from the outside.

A Giant Flagship of Urban Culture

The size of the ICC didn't much concern Zara Pfeifer. Her work as a photographer displays a general interest in very large objects: semitrucks, which she has been following on their journeys through Europe since 2018,[14] or the visionary social housing buildings shaped like oversized waves that architect Harry Glück built in the 1970s in Alt-Erlaa in Vienna's green hinterland.[15]

Öffentlichkeit sehen, dass das Haus im Innern keineswegs so ruinös und verfallen ist, wie es von außen wirken mag.

Ozeanriese der Stadtkultur

Die Größe des ICC hat Zara Pfeifer nicht weiter beeindruckt. Als Fotografin hat sie einen gewissen Hang zu übergroßen Dingen. Zu ihren Themen gehören unter anderem auch Lastwagen, die sie seit 2018 auf ihren Fahrten durch Europa begleitet,[14] oder die visionären Sozialwohnungsbauten, die der Architekt Harry Glück in den 1970er-Jahren wie übergroße Wellen in Alt-Erlaa ins grüne Umland Wiens bauen ließ.[15] Bei ihren Fahrten mit den Lkw taucht Pfeifer für Wochen vollständig in die Welt der großen Maschinen ein, bis ihr die Größe der weiten Parkplätze, der Autobahnen und gigantischen Fähren nicht mehr ganz so gewaltig erscheint. „Wenn man danebensteht", so Pfeifer, „wenn 100 Lkw in den weit offenen Bauch einer riesigen Autofähre fahren, dann kommen einem die Lkw plötzlich ganz klein vor." In Alt-Erlaa hat sie sich vor allem für die Menschen interessiert und dafür, wie diese sich in den Riesenhäusern eingerichtet haben.

Pfeifer erzählt, dass sie sich für diesen übergroßen Maßstab interessiert, wo der Mensch nicht mehr das Maß der Dinge ist – und für die Stellen, an denen sich die Maßstäbe von Mensch und Maschine berühren. Auch im ICC verändert sich die Maschine, sobald man sie betritt. Die Innenwelten sind auf den Menschen ausgerichtet und überall vermitteln bestimmte Elemente zwischen dessen Zerbrechlichkeit und den riesigen Dimensionen der menschgemachten Infrastrukturen draußen vor den Panoramascheiben. Pfeifer sagt, sie habe beim Eintritt ins Innere eine „wohlige, warme Geborgenheit" entdeckt. Genau das zeichnet ihre Aufnahmen meiner Meinung nach aus: Mit einem extrem präzisen und sachlichen Blick entdeckt sie im ICC jene Stellen, an denen sich die Maschine den

Traveling with semis, Pfeifer immerses herself in the world of enormous machines for weeks at a time, until the vast parking lots, the highways, and the gigantic ferries slowly cease to seem so huge. "When you stand next to a massive ferry for vehicles," Pfeifer says, "and watch 100 semitrucks drive into its gaping belly, suddenly they seem quite small." In Alt-Erlaa, she was particularly interested in the people and how they had made homes for themselves in the gargantuan structures.

Pfeifer explains that she is interested in this oversized scale, where human beings are no longer the measure of things—and in the places where human and machine scales intersect. In the ICC, too, the machine changes the moment you enter. Its interior worlds are designed with humans in mind, with specific elements everywhere that mediate between human fragility and the gigantic dimensions of the human-made infrastructure just outside its panoramic windows. Pfeifer says that when she entered the building, she felt a "comforting, warm sense of security." In my opinion, this is exactly what her photographs have captured. With an extremely precise and objective eye, she uncovers those places in the ICC where the machine turns toward its human visitors without denying its own dimensions. The distribution of information desks, coat-checks, and seating areas transforms the interior world into spaces that are absolutely oriented toward human beings despite their generous scale. The escalators are not oversized at all, and with their nearly hallucinogenic patterns the carpets create a soundscape as subdued as the light from outside. There can be no doubt: the ICC is—and can once again be—a people-friendly machine, if only the sleeping giant can finally be turned into a permanently open, vibrant venue for the many kinds of congresses, events, and exhibitions that still happen today. The restrictions imposed during the current coronavirus pandemic have only made us all the more acutely aware of the need for such spaces and their ability to foster direct

Menschen zuwendet, ohne dabei die eigene Größe zu verleugnen. Die Verteilung von Infoschaltern, Garderoben und Sitzmöbeln verwandelt die Innenwelt in zwar besonders großzügige, aber absolut am Menschen orientierte Räume. Die Rolltreppen sind überhaupt nicht übergroß und die Teppiche mit ihren geradezu halluzinogenen Mustern schaffen eine Akustik, die so gedämpft ist wie das Licht von außen. Kein Zweifel: Das ICC ist eine menschenfreundliche Maschine – und kann das wieder werden, wenn es gelingt, aus dem schlafenden Riesen endlich einen dauerhaft geöffneten, lebendigen Ort für die vielfältigen Kongress-, Veranstaltungs- und Ausstellungs-bedürfnisse unserer Gegenwart zu machen. Die Einschränkungen der Corona-Zeiten haben uns die Notwendigkeit solcher Räume, die dem direkten Austausch dienen, nur umso heftiger bewusst gemacht. Pfeifers Aufnahmen haben dabei eine unsentimentale Nüchternheit, die nichts beschönigt. Sie zeigen die Innenwelten des ICC in ihrer faszinierenden Pracht zwischen der Patina des leichten Verfalls durch starken Gebrauch und dem schwachen Leuchten einer verblassenden, vergangenen Zivilisation; denn nichts anderes ist das West-Berlin der 1960er-Jahre heute. Es wäre doch schön, wenn dieses Gebäude erneut in See stechen könnte – als Ozeanriese der Stadtkultur.

exchange. Pfeifer's photographs have an unsentimental tone, a matter-of-fact quality that doesn't embellish what the camera sees. They show the interior worlds of the ICC in their fascinating splendor between the patina of slight decay that has come with the building's heavy use and the faint glow of a fading, bygone civilization—what West Berlin of the 1960s is for us today. How terrific it would be if this building could set sail again—as a giant flagship of urban culture.

1   Ralf Schüler: Bemerkungen der Architekten, in: Bauwelt, Heft 17, Jg. 1979, S. 679
2   Vgl. v. a. Rolf Rave, Hans-Joachim Knöfel, Jan Rave: Bauen der 70er Jahre in Berlin, Berlin: Kiepert 1981; Rolf Rave: Modern Architecture in Berlin, Stuttgart: Edition Axel Menges 2009; Adrian von Buttlar, Kerstin Wittmann-Englert, Gabriele Dolff-Bonekämpfer (Hg.): Baukunst der Nachkriegsmoderne. Architekturführer Berlin 1949–1979, Berlin: Dietrich Reimer Verlag 2013; Berlinische Galerie (Hg.): Radikal Modern: Planen und Bauen im

1   Ralf Schüler, "Bemerkungen der Architekten," Bauwelt 17 (1979): 679.
2   See especially Rolf Rave, Hans-Joachim Knöfel, and Jan Rave, Bauen der 70er Jahre in Berlin (Berlin: Kiepert, 1981), Rolf Rave, Modern Architecture in Berlin (Stuttgart: Edition Axel Menges, 2009); Adrian von Buttlar, Kerstin Wittmann-Englert, and Gabriele Dolff-Bonekämpfer, eds., Baukunst der Nachkriegsmoderne: Architekturführer Berlin 1949–1979 (Berlin: Dietrich Reimer Verlag, 2013); Berlinische Galerie, ed., Radically Modern: Urban Planning and Architecture in 1960s Berlin (Berlin: Wasmuth Verlag, 2015).
3   See Peter Ortner, The Essence of Berlin-Tegel: Taking Stock of an Airport's Architecture, trans. Michael Thomas Taylor (Berlin: jovis, 2020); Jürgen Tietz, ed., TXL: Berlin Tegel Airport (Zurich: Park Books, 2020).
4   Ursulina Schüler-Witte, Ralf Schüler und Ursulina Schüler-Witte: Eine werkorientierte Biografie der Architekten des ICC (Berlin: Lukas Verlag, 2015), 56
5   Ibid.
6   Ibid., 57.
7   Ibid., 61.
8   Ibid., 63.
9   See Berlin.de, "Geisel: ICC-Sanierung könnte teurer werden," May 23, 2016, https://www.berlin.de/

Berlin der 1960er-Jahre, Berlin: Wasmuth Verlag 2015

3 Vgl. Peter Ortner: The Essence of Berlin-Tegel. Taking Stock of an Airport's Architecture, Berlin: jovis 2020; Jürgen Tietz (Hg.): TXL. Berlin Tegel Airport, Zürich: Park Books 2020

4 Ursulina Schüler-Witte: Ralf Schüler und Ursulina Schüler-Witte. Eine werkorientierte Biografie der Architekten des ICC, Berlin: Lukas Verlag 2015, S. 56

5 Ebenda

6 Ebenda, S. 57

7 Ebenda, S. 61

8 Ebenda, S. 63

9 Vgl. Berlin.de: „Geisel: ICC-Sanierung könnte teurer werden", 23. Mai 2016, https://www.berlin.de/aktuelles/berlin/4424842-958092-geisel-iccsanierung-koennte-teurer-werden.html (letzter Aufruf: 24. März 2022)

10 Vgl. Senatsverwaltung für Wirtschaft, Energie und Betriebe: „Sanierung des Internationalen Congress Centrums Berlin (ICC)", 23. Oktober 2019, https://www.parlament-berlin.de/adosservice/18/Haupt/vorgang/h18-2562-v.pdf (letzter Aufruf: 24. März 2022)

11 Vgl. International Center for Contemporary Culture (ICCC), https://iccc.berlin/ (letzter Aufruf: 26. März 2022)

12 Vgl. Berlin.de: „ICC unter Denkmalschutz", https://www.berlin.de/landesdenkmalamt/aktuelles/kurzmeldungen/2019/artikel.842977.php (letzter Aufruf: 26. März 2022)

13 Berliner Festspiele: „The Sun Machine Is Coming Down. Recap", https://www.youtube.com/watch?v=PA9QuPSRu3c (letzter Aufruf: 26. März 2022)

14 Zara Pfeifer: „Good Street!", http://www.zarapfeifer.com/good-street (letzter Aufruf: 26. März 2022)

15 Zara Pfeifer: Du, meine konkrete Utopie: Alterlaa 2013–2017, Bielefeld: Kerber Verlag 2017

aktuelles/berlin/4424842-958092-geisel-iccsanierung-koennte-teurer-werden.html, last accessed March 24, 2022.

10 See Senatsverwaltung für Wirtschaft, Energie und Betriebe, "Sanierung des Internationalen Congress Centrums Berlin (ICC)," October 23, 2019, https://www.parlament-berlin.de/adosservice/18/Haupt/vorgang/h18-2562-v.pdf, last accessed March 24, 2022.

11 See International Center for Contemporary Culture (ICCC), https://iccc.berlin/, last accessed March 26, 2022.

12 See Berlin.de, "ICC unter Denkmalschutz," https://www.berlin.de/landesdenkmalamt/aktuelles/kurzmeldungen/2019/artikel.842977.php, last accessed March 26, 2022.

13 Berliner Festspiele, "The Sun Machine Is Coming Down: Recap," https://www.youtube.com/watch?v=PA9QuPSRu3c, last accessed March 26, 2022.

14 Zara Pfeifer, "Good Street!," http://www.zarapfeifer.com/good-street, last accessed, March 26, 2022.

15 Zara Pfeifer, Du, meine konkrete Utopie: Alterlaa 2013–2017 (Bielefeld: Kerber Verlag, 2017).

KONGRESSZENTRUM BERLIN   QUERSCHNITT DURCH DAS HAUPTGEBÄUDE UND DIE AUSSTELLUNGSHA

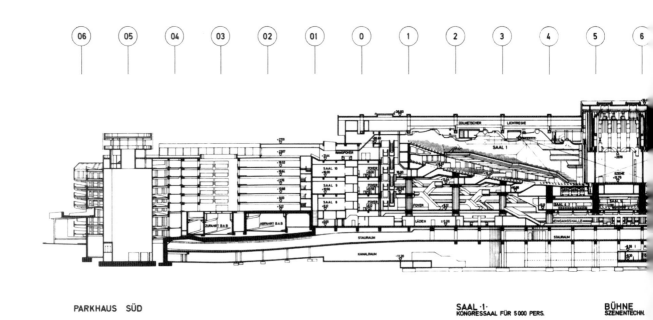

STADTAUTOBAHN   KONGRESSGEBÄUDE   MESSEDAMM   ÜBERGANGSBAUWERK   AUSSTELLUNGSHALLEN

06 05 04 03 02 01 0 1 2 3 4 5 6

PARKHAUS SÜD   SAAL ·1·   BÜHNE
                                            KONGRESSAAL FÜR 5000 PERS.   SZENENTECHN.

BAUHERR: BERLINER AUSSTELLUNGEN
ARCHITEKTEN: RALF SCHÜLER, DIPL.ING. URSULINA WITTE
HAUPTÜBERNEHMER: NEUE HEIMAT STÄDTEBAU, HAMBURG
INGENIEURPLANUNG
ALS NEBENÜBERNEHMER: GERHARD BARTELS

1 EINGANGSHALLE
2 MITTELFOYER 1
3 MITTELFOYER 2
4 BANKETTSAAL
5 PROJEKTIONSKABINE
6 LICHTREGIE
7 BANKETTSAALFOYER
8 RANG SAAL 2
9 SIMULTANKABINE
10 SPRECHERKABINE
11 SEITENFOYER OST
12 TAGUNGSBÜRO
13 GALERIE 1, 2
14 GARDEROBE – WC
15 KLIMAZENTRALE
16 BIO – MÜLLTANK
17 MÜLLRAUM
18 HAUSLAGER
19 KANALRAUM
20 STADRAUM
21 TECHN. ZENTRALE
22 HAUSTECHNIK – KELLER
23 AUSSTELLUNGSHALLE
24 AUSSTELLUNGSHALLE

FUNKTURM

LÄNGSSCHNITT

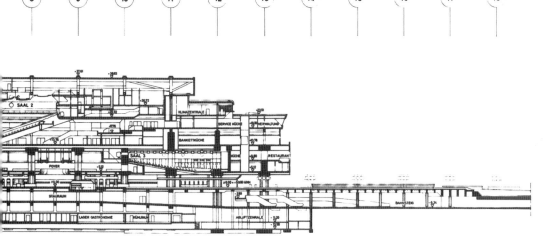

SAAL ·2·
BANKETTSAAL FÜR 3000 PERS.

VORPLATZ

Impressum

© 2022 by jovis Verlag GmbH
Das Copyright für die Texte liegt
bei Florian Heilmeyer
Das Copyright für die Fotografien liegt
bei Zara Pfeifer

Umschlagmotiv: Zara Pfeifer
Lektorat: Theresa Hartherz
Design: Something Fantastic A.D.
Layout und Satz: Susanne Rösler
Lithografie: Bild1Druck
Gedruckt in der Europäischen Union

Bibliografische Information der Deutschen
Nationalbibliothek:
Die Deutsche Nationalbibliothek
verzeichnet diese Publikation in der
Deutschen Nationalbibliografie; detaillierte
bibliografische Daten sind im Internet über
http://dnb.d-nb.de abrufbar

jovis Verlag GmbH
Lützowstraße 33
10785 Berlin

www.jovis.de

jovis-Bücher sind weltweit im ausgewählten
Buchhandel erhältlich. Informationen zu
unserem internationalen Vertrieb erhalten
Sie von Ihrem Buchhändler oder unter
www.jovis.de

ISBN 978-3-86859-756-1

Colophon

© 2022 by jovis Verlag GmbH
Texts by kind permission
of Florian Heilmeyer
Photographs by kind permission
of Zara Pfeifer

Cover image: Zara Pfeifer
Translation into English:
Michael Thomas Taylor
Copy-editing: Michael Thomas Taylor
Design: Something Fantastic A.D.
Layout and setting: Susanne Rösler
Lithography: Bild1Druck
Printed in the European Union

Bibliographic information published by the
Deutsche Nationalbibliothek:
The Deutsche Nationalbibliothek
lists this publication in the Deutsche
Nationalbibliografie; detailed bibliographic
data are available on the Internet at
http://dnb.d-nb.de

jovis Verlag GmbH
Lützowstraße 33
10785 Berlin

www.jovis.de

jovis books are available worldwide in
select bookstores. Please contact your
nearest bookseller or visit www.jovis.de
for information concerning your local
distribution

ISBN 978-3-86859-756-1